# The Wright Legacy Vol. 1:

# The Proposal

Phoenix Garrett Wright

I dedicate this book to you, Grandma. For all the parts of you that were curious and true, this is your return on that investment.

*Piano*..............................................................................*pg.7*

*Don't Know What To Feel*...........................................................*pg.9*

*Friendship*......................................................................*pg.10*

*From Scratch*..................................................................*pg.11*

*Secret Places*..................................................................*pg.12*

*I Meant To Say*...............................................................*pg.13*

*You'll Never Leave*..........................................................*pg.14*

*Letters*.........................................................................*pg.15*

*This Is Sex.........pg.17*

*Vent*....................................................................*pg.18*

*Where Do We Go From Here*....................................................*pg.19*

*I Wished She Loved Me*.......................................................*pg.20*

*The Way It Feels*.............................................................*pg.21*

*Friend To Me*.................................................................*pg.22*

*Beggars Throne*..............................................................*pg.23*

*The Color of Air*.............................................................*pg.24*

*Kiss of Cancer*...............................................................*pg.25*

*Our Together Unknown*....................................................*pg.26*

End Your Affection...............pg.27

Don't Know Why I Do These Things...............pg.28

Women...............pg.30

Small Gospel...............pg.32

Mamma Would've Been Proud...............pg.33

Satellite...............pg.34

Supposed To Be...............pg.35

Unbalanced...............pg.36

Unconnected Thoughts of Loneliness.........pg.37

Blown Out Candles...............pg.38

Never Be...............pg.40

Traces of Where I Have Been...............pg.41

Call...............pg.42

Last Addiction...............pg.43

Natural...............pg.44

I've Changed...............pg.46

In A Woman...............pg.48

Introvert Extrovert...............pg.49

*Not All About Love……..…………………………………..….pg.50*

*Winter Melody………………………………………....…pg.51*

*Song Bird………………………………………….…..……pg.52*

*Chances Are…………………………………………….pg.53*

*Godsend………………………………………………………..pg.55*

*Journal For Me- Day 3……………………………………………………pg.56*

*Journal For Me- Day 4……………………………………………...pg.57*

*Give You Everything………………………………………...pg.58*

*How Did I…………………………………………….pg.60*

*Shades of My Past……………………………………………..pg.61*

*When Heaven Calls……………………………………………...…pg.62*

*Every Day I'm Dying………………………………………………...pg.64*

*Call My Name………………………………………………...pg.65*

*I'm Ready Now………………………………………………...pg.67*

*Dreaming About Love…………………………………………...pg.69*

*Where Do I Begin……………………………………………...pg.70*

*Afraid To Love…………………………………………...pg.71*

*My Divinity………………………………………………pg.72*

*You Can Believe in Me*..................................................................pg.73

*Matter To You*..................................................................pg.75

*I'm So In Love*..................................................................pg.76

*Let's Make Love*..................................................................pg.77

*Wild Flowers*..................................................................pg.78

*Destiny Has Done Its Part*..................................................................pg.79

*The Proposal*..................................................................pg.80

She sat at her brown baby grand

Petting the zebra keys

While she read the notes

Illuminated by a yellow lamp,

Photographs, books, antiques equally yellow

With age surrounding her like a silver cage

Annotating the time spent between

Being a woman, losing a girl,

And certain pains taming her spirit,

Not unlike the diabetes restricting her body

From eating what it wants to,

She used to pull emotion from the world

Like an infant from the womb,

And warm tears was your joy from her lyrics,

Now, she just hums her notes

One finger removed from middle C

She sat at her brown baby grand
Petting the zebra keys
While she read the notes
Illuminated by a yellow lamp,
Photographs, books, antiques equally yellow
With age surrounding her like a Silver Cage
Annotating the time spent between
Being a woman, losing a girl,
And certain ~~parts~~ pains taming her spirit,
Not unlike the diabetes restricting her body
From eating what it wants to,
She used to pull emotion from the world
Like an infant from the womb,
And warm tears was your joy from her lyrics,
Now, she just hums her notes,
One finger removed from middle C

Today, I want to be alone with my feelings

Except, I don't know what to feel,

I'm cornered by emptiness

Yet, uninhibited by emotion

I'm a soap bubble

Created by the breath of a child

To float until I burst

Amongst cumulus clouds,

I could detail my life

But what would it be-

A couple of lines or pages

In a locked diary,

I'm a loner by nature

Because closeness bothers me,

I'm the sweaty palm

People are eager to let go of,

So I'd rather keep my hands to myself

As well as my love,

I'm a Mute Swan floating on a pond

Disturbing the water around a pair of doves

It's hard for me to judge how much I've grown
When spiritual maturity cannot be measured
By yard sticks or light years,
Though I know I've made divisions of myself
Times when I crawled over obstacles of granite
To shed one external layer for another…
Until I strip away every superficial rind
Those innate beauties that surface in words periodically
Shall remain a distant nature, mysterious
As a forested habitat, explored but uncharted,
Campfires of friendship, some eternally burning,
Others still warm, but left in ashes
To mark a trail that can only be traced in memory,
Yet, with each cinder, or amber of every new flame
That forested space bound only by introverted emptiness
Will forever expand

I think we were both casual consumers of beauty
Decimated that our hearts were pillaged cities
With starving citizens, we were life's bottom feeders,
Searching the heavens for the answers,
And instead finding each other
Wrapped in blankets of insecurity,
Not only unsure of ourselves,
But unsure of what others could see in us,
So we walked that dirty path together,
Ashamed to feel anything for anyone,
Even for each other,
We directed compliments to clothes or accessories,
"Those are nice shoes,"
"You have beautiful earrings,"
"What cologne is that, it smells good,"
But these were minor attempts
To salvage lands littered with neglect,
However, it was a start- a new beginning,
A snapshot of a horizon over in the distance
With two silhouettes atop a hill
Adjoined shoulder to shoulder
Waiting for the oncoming sun

It's in those secret places we meet

By the concrete steps under the bridge,

Or in my small apartment

Away from curious eyes that confuses me

That makes me think of a larger purpose,

Or greater scheme,

It's in the corner of buildings in public places

And behind my bedroom door

That minimizes the grand plan

And focuses on the smaller element of you and I

Why are we sneaking around,

Why do we bury this secret so deep in our hearts

We barely acknowledge each other's presence,

In the company of others there is a grave silence

And I resist the eye-contact you try to steal,

My soul recedes into its own secret place

Beyond the blank stare of my facial expression,

Where can I hide,

It seems no place is safe from love,

Because I woke up this morning and you were there

Still looking at me,

Still not willing to give up,

Even when I retreat to my secret places

Your kiss penetrates every layer

Steam arose from our coco into cream coated nostrils
Warmth starting to nudge me past small coy sips,
As we people watch through the great pane of glass,
A fraternal mirror to those outside wanting to glance in,
Pedestrians lucky enough to be drawn in by your smile
Take happiness to their hearts like a secret to the grave,
But my spirit would linger on these cobblestone streets
If you died today, in this way- in love and unknowing,
We've spoken on truth before, I watched your lips move,
And I agreed that it was not wise to speak falsely,
So I let the reverence of our friendship manifest wildly
I'd fall asleep with my head nestled in your cleavage,
Or I'd wait until the day's tension compressed your spine
To progressively run my hands the full length of your body,
You wrapped inklings of romance in hugs I didn't deserve
And I accepted them a little too tightly for misinterpretation,
Edging back from the table, I laid a few dollars by our cups,
Insufficient reparations for all the time that I have stolen,
But time too enjoyable to adulterate my palate for romance,
Yet, everyday I've been meaning to say, I'm in love with her...

The one girl I can't have manifests in every feminine image
I cast my eyes on, as if your living soul haunts my vision,
And the kiss I placed on the girl I loved was felt by her,
But was an experience I shared with you,
And her name too became yours
In passionate moments spent between her left and right thigh,
With deeper strokes aimed at reaching the vale of her body
Grinding my way into the marrow of your being,
I always find myself in the midst of ambient light
Glowing in vibrant storms of brown
Exquisite as the complexion of your skin,
Your face the dawn of my daybreak,
And the water that ripples in the basin of yesterday
Is caused by the feet you used to walk in my life,
Now my every step traces back to the first moment I met you,
Where I was in love then as I am now,
Knowing in both epochs
That you will linger in eternity, dually
Drifting in the orbit of my conscious
And anchoring the gravity of my mind's eye

Small parcel, brown package
All my letters returned to me
Unopened, unwanted, unbelievable
I could share my feelings with you
And it wasn't worth
The stamps I put on the envelopes,
Wait, here's a letter from you
    How can you feel so passionate
    For someone you don't know
    You marry ideals,
    And love is not you telling me so,
    I'm not the woman you think I am,
    And I'm not the woman you want me to be
    I'm an everyday woman,
    Not your fantasy, your fairytale,
    And I'm not one for doing favors,
    But you can do one for me,
    Forget I ever existed, and happiness will be yours,
    Because then you'll find someone you really care for
After her last word I closed her letter
And a chapter to my life,
But dog-eared the page,
Highlighting the words that read,
Sincerely Yours

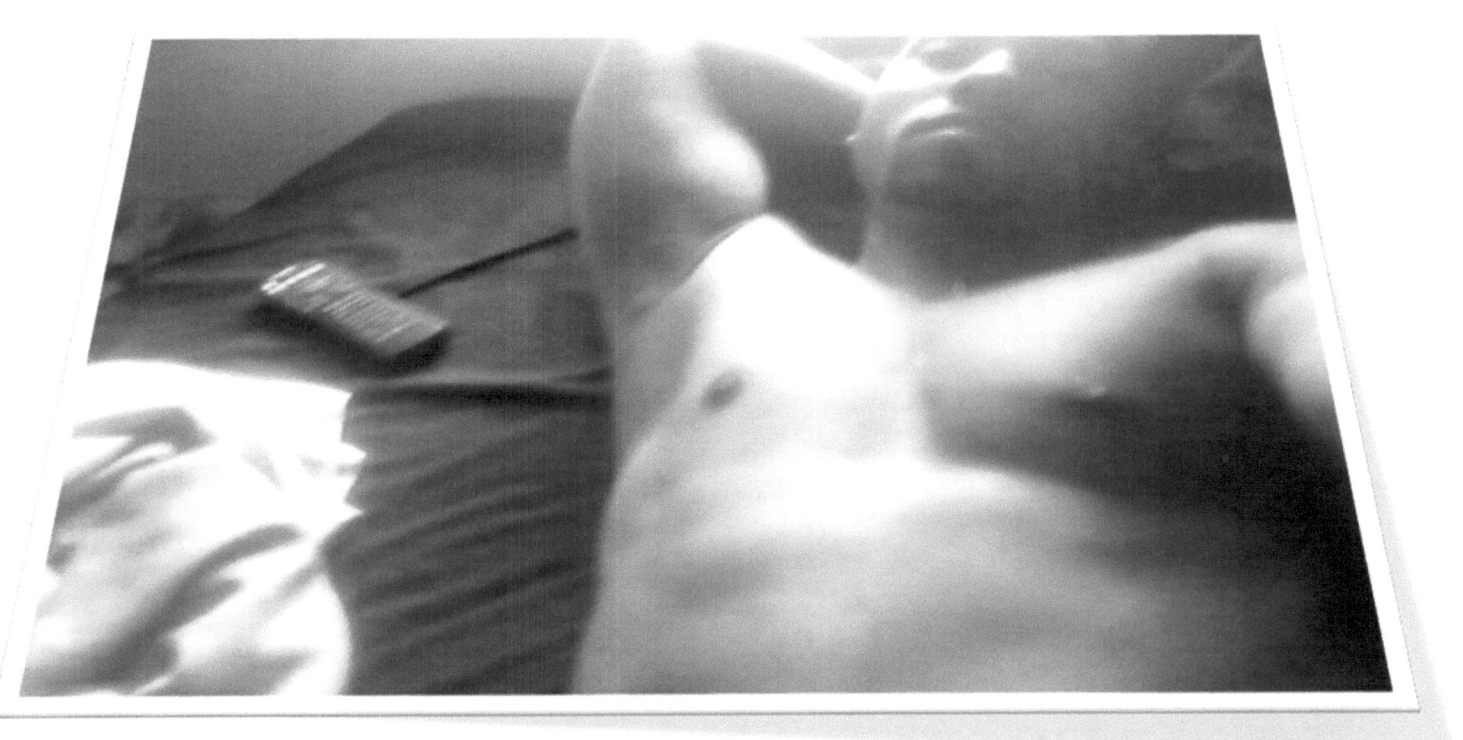

*Black lights peek from the four corners of the room*
*For we are at the center of this ultraviolet universe,*
*Within seconds of the start of our creation, skin exposed,*
*Nipples hard to the hum of my AC, and maybe this cube of ice*
*Melting on your areola, as I lick water running down your breast*
*Into your cleavage, tasting the salt in the surf of your heartbeat,*
*Putting my hand on your other gland so no parts of you are lonely,*
*But this is only sex- no feelings, no hurt, no strings attached,*
*Just the streams of saliva you have carefully wrapped*
*Around my golden girth with your tan lips*
*And I'm going to kiss you still, because real women suck dick,*
*I take comfort in your acknowledgment and sincere recognition,*
*Expounding upon that knowledge like you authored it*
*Taking sips of my juices in-between chapters as we change scenes,*
*Because This Is Sex, not just the fixation of an oral poet...*

*With a focused hand I scrape condoms from my night stand*
*Studded, Ribbed, Shared Pleasure, or Warm Sensation-*
*Sort of like the way my finger feels at the equator of your body*
*Searching for the paradise of your plump g-spot,*
*It's like the sponge we use in your bubble bath*
*As I apply pressure to your skin with circular strokes,*
*We're getting close, as you hope this last the night,*
*Or at least an hour, maybe two, because This Is Sex,*
*Not 30 second porn clips from tnaflix.com- I do research,*
*Pillows under your waistline, cameras on for face time,*
*Hot oils across the spine, down your crack,*
*And onto my manhood as I enter you from the back-*
*Baby, I'm a sexpert, I'll show you how sex works*
*To enhance your mood, drop some pounds,*
*And develop your vocabulary so that when in conversation,*
*You can say something like, babydisisthemuthafuckinshit,*
*You know, multi-syllabic...yes, I'm an addict, but This Is Sex*

*You seem to float on air as you ride just the tip of my penis*
*Interrupting fantasy of cunnilingus with whip cream and blueberries*
*Trying to stay mentally strong about my doctor's decision for circumcision*
*And the added bliss I feel towards the top of my shaft,*
*I grab your ass cheeks and spread them apart, then push them together*
*Like a black accordion, making the music that my skin flute dreamed*
*When I was younger, using Vaseline in Glad Bags in-between mattresses,*
*You know what they say about idle minds, and I had a lot time to practice,*
*So you can experience the magic of talent and hard work coming together*
*For your pleasure, because This Is Sex- X-Rated but also underrated,*
*Never overstated, This is SEx...also available over the counter*

Cold air surged through the dusty overhead vent
As if it were going to deter humidity from rising,
But it was too late, her bedroom sweltered passion,
Beads of precipitation mounted the canary walls,
Cream sheets formed small tides of scented moisture
That leeched various body parts with each roll or turn,
Her top lip clung to my bottom lip before losing grasp
Falling past the cliff of my chin to the bottom of my chest
Pink lipstick smeared all over rocky abdominal muscles,
Her hair strewn in so many directions I lost sight of her,
But not her touch, cataloguing each nerve below my waist,
Her fingernails knifing small circles around each visible vein,
Her tongue parachuting down the long length of my shaft
Saliva building in anticipation of joining a much larger lagoon,
And from the abyss she emerged on top of me ready for more,
For more warmth, for more heat, for more sanguine exposure,
Her flush blood adrenaline rushed throughout her honey skin
As she rode my body into the coils of the king sized mattress,
Sweat dripped off the slope of her breast and sizzled on my body,
Straining to reach the vent, my hand limp over my broken head

Her head and back were off the bed, hands on the floor
Candy Cane colored stockings, waist on the edge
In-between her legs there was no hair at all
Just a beautiful space to put my face...and slowly lick,
I've never tasted a clit so sweet, rubbing it on my lips,
Giving it a little tug, a little pull, sucking it and pressing in,
Goddamn...I felt her thighs tremble on my cheekbones
I lowered the angle of my tongue, as her hips raised,
And unfazed I went in, round and round her liquid walls
Until I paused- taking my tongue's tip gently to her clit- again,
It's sin in her heartbeat, blood sizzling in her veins
And she's straining to come up with words to match the moment
So she just moans and grabs my head with her small hands
Wondering what's next, and if she will let me go all the way,
But I see it in her light brown eyes, it's no longer about my tongue,
It's all about her coming.........coming to her senses,
Because I'm not her boyfriend, I'm just a really good friend
That caught her in a fragile position, and she's been hurt before
So she scoots back to the floor and asks me where we go from here

It would be different if she never knew I existed,
If the council of her thoughts burned like an oil lamp
Swaying through the world's various midnights,
And only her Lumina pinched darkness to sparks,
But as she imagines a greater purpose of a life fulfilled
I sail through her evolving universe like a rouge star,
And though she has been unable to chart a flight pattern
She knows that something always brings me back to her,
Yet, what that is, she knows not- nor will I ever tell her,
Just as she will never tell me the one thing I want to hear,
If she would say...If she would just tell me at least once...
"I Love You"...but I will never hear her say those words,
Because she never says anything that she does not mean,
And I wouldn't have it any other way, except to say,
It's hard for me to be close to her because I know myself,
And the way she sees life, as a tangible dream to pursue,
Will lead her to believe that all she has to do is try,
So she limits her thoughts of me as I move past her,
As I look back wondering if she'll waste a wish on love

This is the way it feels when you have no one at all,
You look at your phones though no one calls,
And you wonder why you pay a bill for just in case,
Or you slowly eat a meal at a restaurant with two chairs,
But no one joins you or even watches you eat,
You order desert just to take up more time before sleep
Filling your day with calories instead of depression;
Sure was a yummy fudge brownie- false smiles,
You take pictures of crumbs, and try to give your life meaning
I was there, and it was great times,
And then you remind yourself- it was just me,
And you realize you have photo albums with days and events
But they were just Polaroids with no one in it
2 gigabytes of digital emptiness saved on disk
The life you've lived, a Sanyo to bear witness...
How many nights, full moons, and extinguished stars
Have you spent awake curled up on your side
With no one on the other side of you,
Just an empty space on a clean bedspread,
So you spoon with your heart hoping you feel love

I saw a country sky fold itself up at dawn
Dropping a single orange star out its bundle,
And recede back into the thicket of the universe,
Waiting again to cover me with its nightly wonder,
I'm a city boy still in awe of unpolluted celestial sights
Not downloaded from the internet on my cell phone,
A breath of fresh air can be smelled on small stones,
And the girth of a tree is like an infant holding its fathers leg,
It seems like nature left the city and the suburbs long ago
Settling instead for quiet reservations across the globe,
Where polar bears can skate in the nude on icebergs,
Or an entire forest is a log cabin to birds like spotted owls,
I've seen blades of grass suffer in the confines of concrete,
Stars wallow in the filth of a row of sorted streetlights,
I've seen a plant in a pot of dirt with its roots hung from holes
While its brown leaves limp over the brim to escape that fate,
But out here it is different, the moon sits on mountain peaks,
The wind plays with the trees, the sun is an oracle to the sand,
And nature is a close friend to me...listen...it's in that canyon,
An echo of my sentiments...a close friend to me, a close friend to me

She came to my throne as a beggar
Garments shredded seductively
Holes ripped in her blue jeans
Near her inner thigh and below her left cheek,
Her grey eyes were like tiny dream catchers
Knowing the weaknesses of my sovereignty
Playing into her own vices, this tragic grip
That held on the to the both of us, like a pair of lips,
She kissed the tip of my scepter,
Left a subtle shine to my crown,
Knowledge of her was incredible
And she was just a girl from a small town,
But I erect monuments of her while under spell of night,
And during the release of morning I call her name,
Regrettably, she had to leave...
But I was glad that I came

Have you seen the color of air

Purple as a plum, but soft as a pastel,

How dazed you must feel, unbalanced,

Unfocused, equilibrium intoxicated,

A sun spotted spectrum of dots

Like when you close your eyes too tight,

This violet dawn, romance drawn

Like lipstick on a thin lipped horizon...

I've kissed you before,

And love passed through me,

As if I was a body of water

Streamlined by a dipped hand

What could you have taken,

What could you have placed within...

I felt once, as if someone lived inside of me

Talking at an even pace, as I remained quiet,

Telling me things would be ok, and they would stay,

As needed, but eventually they would pass away

Beyond thoughts of what is and isn't fair,

Marooned to the transparent color of air

You kiss of cancer, slowly debilitating- crippling

You methodically take my life away,

With every touch of your lips my soul slips

Like the fall of your hand away from my cheek,

As if that soft caress, that gentle rub, could ignite like ether

And burn through every pore until my heart was no more

Even though we're reflections, divided is all we'll ever be
Just as if you were a star and I was the sea,
Sometimes on a clear night, I will see you within me
Light breeding in currents while treading water to breathe

Love would be a strange feeling
If happiness were an antagonist
Jostling its steps for the merriment of sorrow,
And so seems my love for you- a strange feeling,
Without thought or reservation, we make love,
The soft motion of your lips sliding slowly down
The sugary veins on the right side of my neck...
My bloodline is decadent, an unyielding spirit,
And, yet, we laugh throughout the day's torment,
I know you aren't meant to last, but you're here,
Peering deep into the destruction that is you
Not caring that what I see is a fallible trust
You've promised that you'll always be around,
But sometimes a lie is told when truth sounds good,
And even as you hold my hand while I look at you,
The pleasure of your palm is a sweaty reminder
That I am too nervous to continue living for the day
That you'd end your affection, so today I walk away

I don't know why I do these things,
Give you hope of a you and me,
There is no such thing, there is only me,
How selfish indeed, little Indian Giver,
My life you won't understand,
Full of irrational decisions based on temptation,
Greed, desire, lust, abstraction after abstraction
Right down to the tangible touch of your satin G-string
And moistened opening of your vaginal candy land,
More like a honey pot to my sticky fingers
Sweet flavoring to my tongues delight,
But behind this body is a woman who cares for me
To the point of ridicule from those who care for her,
Not me; I've told you before, what loves been like
This corridor of flickering lights, giving a glimmer
Of perpetual waste smeared throughout this narrow hall,
I'm a resident who's never been to the end of either end,
Stuck in the middle, this familiar place of your clitoral landmark,
I am beautiful, so says this truth inside of me,
But I don't know why I do these things...help me

T̶h̶e̶ ̶m̶a̶g̶i̶c̶

T . . . . . . . do these things,
Give you hope of a you and me
There is no such thing, there is only me,
How selfish indeed, little indian-giver,
My life you won't understand,
Full of irrational decisions based on temptation,
Greed, desire, lust, abstraction after abstraction
Right down to the tangible touch of your satin g-string
And moistened opening of your vaginal candy land,
~~More ~~~~~~~~~~~~~~~~~~~~~~~~~~~~~~~~
More like a honey pot to my sticky fingers
Sweet flavoring to my tongue's delight,
But behind this body is a woman who cares for me
To the point of ridicule from those who care for her,
Not me; I've told you before, what love's been like
This corridor of flickering lights, giving a glimmer
Of perpetual waste smeared throughout this narrow hall,
I'm a resident who's never been to the end of either end
Stuck in the middle, this familiar place of your clitoral landmark,
I am beautiful, so says this truth inside of me,
But I don't know why I do these things... help me

Been around the world  
Via valleys of different women  
Learned cultural divisions  
Through the crease of bed linens &  
Differences in religion,  
They pray to the lord,  
I pray I don't get bored  
With this morsel of heaven,  
I can't help but want more

You're a small gospel that funnels to my heart through my brown eyes,
As you enter the room, people clamor around you awaiting your words
Like you're the physical manifestation of the good news,
Sweet greetings flying from your lips, as if your tongue's a carrier for inspiration
Dispensing fleets of "Hey loves" and "How are you gorgeous?"
It's a feeling of being rewarded for doing nothing at all, but being human,
The courtesy of acknowledging life with bright eyes and visible interest,
Your hugs are more like garments for the spirit, than cues for conversation,
And you initiate them with the ease of a step forward and enclosure of wingspan;
To be housed by your flesh, take your scent, and be touched by your life
Is something of scripture but defies description, it's just a psalm of my love,
But I'm not a part of that inner circle of warm gestures and symmetry of affection
I'm an aficionado based on distant observation and third party information,
Yet, through my own admissions, you know me well,
Because I have inked my reservoir of emotions through the freedom of verse,
And when you glance at me with the acumen of my thoughts on your mind
You must find it odd that I chose to recoil from your offer of friendship
Than embrace the permanent place that you had reserved in your life for me,
You wink at me, as I close my eyes to you, taunting me with your kindness-
Knowing the hardest thing to accept is that I want you, but you don't want my love

Right hand pulls door handle
Left hand escorts her inside
Mama would be proud of this gentleman,
Even if his eyes did wander to her backside...
An actual restaurant- tablecloth, candlelight,
Pulls out her chair, no plastic booths,
Compliments- hair, smile, perfume,
Evening gown was the only thing flawed,
Because "you can't put a price tag on a beautiful woman"
Yes, mama would have been proud of him...
He lets her hand rest in his palm as they eat,
Never mentions sex- just the arts, world views, literature,
And which desert would make her the happiest:
The Strawberry Cheesecake or Lemon Meringue Pie,
Momma would have definitely been proud...
He picked up the check, tipped, and thanked the waiter by name,
Opened the door for her again, as he waited for the valet
To bring around his black Tahoe to help her step inside,
And as he closed his door to drive away, kissed her gently...
I took notes enviously picturing myself in his tailored tux,
Because I know mama would have been proud of me

The humidity was uncomfortable, sweat seeped from my pores,
And the sheets were more of a nuisance than a comfort to me,
Tonight was supposed to be a simple slumber, head to pillow,
Eyelids shut, the day forgotten as tomorrow is invented in dreams,
But here in this singular spot, I'm a satellite under starlight
Open to the universe, patiently waiting on a signal from you...
Unrest has settled in, as I put my back against the headboard,
I search the room for something to do-
Videogames, piano keys, Lego set, Bonsai plant, or turkey sandwich?
I neglect hunger, as I pull this soft down close to my stomach
Holding this feathered substitute with the same candor as I would your frame
But it's just not the same, so I discard the fraudulent offender into a mess of sheets,
Edging near the end of the bed, I put two feet to the ground, and open balcony doors
The cool air places little goose bumps on my skin, as I look for where you might be,
Detroit, Atlanta, New York, Los Angeles, or somewhere in the Chi
I wonder why I allowed myself to be just another guy to see your face
But not know your life: the things you've done, places you've been,
People you've loved- the failures of the heart, of which I've had many,
None greater than you; I cruise through a constellation oaring with rue
Stirring time with my memories, interrupting the night, adjusting my satellite

It was supposed to be enough that I was ready,

Because you after all were waiting on me,

And that idea wasn't romantic,

It was just natural- a supposed to be,

But I was younger then,

The world was conquerable, and I was its hero,

Now I've exchanged my cape for a blue collar

In prelude to a more simple life,

And it was supposed to be easy to whisk you away

From wherever I left you last,

Frozen you would be- in time

But it's only your shoulder that has a touch of frost,

And you won't allow my lips the warmth of yours,

For I know your heart lives in a different climate,

As love experiences a seasonal change,

I sit on an island waiting for rain,

Waiting for rainbows-

But the wind blows a subtle gust

As I exhale a little wind, thinking where did you go,

Where have you been...where are you supposed to be

The sun flew in different directions,
As I struggled with my equilibrium,
I forgot how brutal the morning could be,
As I stand without you able to balance me,
Your large smile on the side of my cheek,
As you once embraced me, faithfully,
And I sort of collapsed unable to stay awake
Incapable of fully appreciating this dream,
Yawing on your love, getting ready for work,
Skipping over breakfast, passing over you,
The most important part of my day, yet,
You stayed, and still I pushed further away,
Taking until the pendulum of this morning
For me to realize life was the equator
From which we once sat to see the world,
And no matter if we fished amongst the stars
To feast on the beauty of night, or
Threw darts at the sun, pointless as it may be
You were there with me, there for me,
And there I linger, staggering towards the blinds

Without quill of ink or pencil of lead
I express emptiness with a voice unsaid
Like a child with a plate left unfed
Belly full of air left for dead

How do you show someone a void,
Or mime emptiness-
When is a tear nothing more than saltwater
Evaporated in a shallow pore,
Where is something lost, found
If feared to be lost once more

Do you know love's like a pathogen
Multiplying silently in my heart,
And you murmur chaos like white noise
Echoed repeatedly in the dark

It's as if I am lying on sand,
And waves are crashing hard on land,
While you as a bird look at me as a man
Thinking I am the source of this paradise
When I wish I could ride your wings
Telling you the sky is life I always dreamed

Ice Cream Cake- Oreo and 3 layers
*"Happy Birthday, Phoenix"* in signature font
28 candles, one for every year since birth
Each flame highlighting my smile,
I inhale a deep breath, and close my eyes...
For every shooting star, or penny in fountain,
Let every positive and selfless wish come true,
And if there is enough magic left in the world
Then I wish for friendship knotted to attraction
Attraction bound to a woman
A woman that is captivated by me
And a small amount of beauty delivered by spirit,
I'm not wishing for love, but for a chance to be in it,
I'm not asking for right away, just an eventually,
Just an eventually I repeat to myself, as I exhale,
Extinguishing flame to vapor with a single breath,
I rest my chin in my right palm pondering the years,
And with a guilty finger swipe the left corner of icing,
Delicious...I look down at the blown out candles
Wondering if I'll have someone to celebrate with next year

## Blowout The Candles

~~Most men won't talk about it, and I'm no different about mine.~~

1) Ice Cream Cake - Oreo and 3 layers
2) Happy Birthday Phoenix in signature font
3) 28 candles, one for every year since birth
4) Each tiny flame highlighting my smile,
5) I inhale a deep breath, and close my eyes...
6) For every shooting star, or penny in a fountain,
7) Let every positive and selfless wish come true
8) ~~~~ And if there is enough magic left in the world
9) Then I wish for friendship knotted to attraction
10) Attraction bound to a woman,
11) A woman that is captivated by me
12) And a small amount of beauty delivered by spirit,
13) I'm not wishing for love, but a chance to be in it
14) I'm not asking for right away, just an eventually
~~~~
15) Just an eventually I repeat to myself, as I exhale,
16) Extinguishing flame to vapor with a single breath,
17) I rest my chin in my right palm pondering the years
~~~~
18) And with a guilty finger swipe the left corner of icing
19) Delicious... I look down at the blownout candles,
20) Wondering if I'll have someone to celebrate with next year

I'll never be the guy that greets the morning with jubilation,
Though a prayer will be said, and appreciation will be felt,
Because my work is not done, and every day I make progress,
For Christ spent 23 years calling to my heart before I answered,
And if I died before then, and failed to amend the constitution
Of my spirit, I would have told you, a Christian- I'll never be,
That thought settles in the creases of my memories time to time,
Especially, as I muse on love, and women of quality I left behind
I'm a star gazer, night flyer, scenery observer, purveyor of good
With a curious pair of eyes, a soft pair of lips, and one working ear
That hears better than it listens, not to mention a mouth so sweet
Hearts flutter when touched by words spoken of a sugar cane tongue,
Yet, sometimes I prefer the divergence of silence to deviance of noise,
And I recoil into the times that I wrote a girl a note, or got a number,
Though was too scared to call, and all I had was the best of intentions
To treat her right, to acknowledge her life, to right wrongs she incurred,
Because I believed in honesty and loyalty first- and I still do, I still do
Hold that belief like a bible in hand that I will be the man I've yet to be,
Too caught up in fantasy- nice smiles, long hair, light skin so smooth
It would seem airbrushed; soft curves, kind words, light eyes,
And the right size to hold in my arms as she holds my hand in hers-
Yes, I've had that before, prayers that were answered, blessings bestowed,
Love forsaken, because relationships grow old and I lack imagination
To reinvent myself or try again, knowing that I'm searching for better,
But it's the optimist in me, that prays for one more blessing, one last chance
To know love again, because if not, then I know that it will never be…

I smudged the tear on her chest into a small wet spot with my thumb,
As she called my name out softly, and asked me what was the matter,
I gave her a simple shrug of the shoulders, as I avoided her eyes,
Instead, I looked at the tender fullness of her lips and touched her cheek,
Knowing she wouldn't understand the intricate details of a man's heart,
And how nice it felt to rest against the warmth of her body in silence,
With the exception of an oscillating space heater and her steady heartbeat,
There was a calm in her breathing, brushing her hand over my bald head,
A harmonious union between my thoughts and the acumen of what was needed-
Someone to unknot the million miles of cognitive congestion that's been building,
Yet, now I sit here, adding more road to an already worn path, wondering....
What is love supposed to feel like if what we just did meant nothing at all,
Her top and bottom lip submerged into mine, tasting the lifeline of happiness,
The cherry flavor of her lip-gloss leaving traces of where she has been,
Her unique sweetness firmly marinated in my ever-changing taste buds,
My top half, her bottom half, the clasping of her legs around my face,
The space in the middle of her body I filled with an engorged mass
A last gasp she was able to muster before her body caved into soaked sheets,
These are the hollow memories that I will never be able to fill with love
She is the woman I have shared everything with, but want nothing from

Sometimes I think I don't have any friends,
And the days pass by with wayward movements
Expressed by the fall of dust or sloth of the second hand,
Different lives I have been part of,
Private moments that seem to die with the years,
Recounted only in my memory- to most I have passed away,
Lost to the newness of the world I left in my childhood,
Because I was made to grow-up too quick,
I've searched for love as deep as the ocean floor,
Finding only a pearl or two,
Never the treasure that brings light to that mysterious depth,
Which permeates life with the strange awareness-
This life is not meant to be lived alone,
And in the shelter of my home,
I sit away from the TV, a great distance from any books,
And light black cherry candles to provide heat for my room,
And I sit and I sit, and I wait and I wait,
Knowing one day, you'll find me in your thoughts and call

You may not understand, but I need to do this for me,
And you might question the morality of my decision,
But I have already decided to make matters worse
Before they get better, because this is my last addiction,
Seeing her undress across from this paltry desk lamp
Small fingers peeling a black leotard from her toned legs,
Her eyes glancing up towards the curiosity of mine,
Smiling at my heart's falsetto giving rise in my jeans,
Something that I don't even try to conceal, similar to you,
Standing there talking to me while removing your t-shirt,
A thin black bra concealing the last mound of flesh
On your otherwise naked upper body, whispering to me,
That those sheer panties need not be worn to the shower,
Her, turning away to go to the bathroom as I lie on her bed,
Beautiful round cheeks slowly slinky up and down
Her head giving a half turn to see if I'm watching-
Why wouldn't I, this is my addiction, I'm a fiend for you,
I think to myself, as you clean your body,
Water traveling different courses from forehead to feet,
Soap lathering in places that I shall one day press my lips,
Satisfaction boring into my taste buds, as I lick your inner thigh
Unable to deny my attraction, which is only partly to you,
I'm thinking this is the last time that I will be able to do this,
This dance, unlike yours- jazz, tap, or classical,
No, this is a slow dance of foreplay, intermittent dialogue,
And forceful motions against the grain of your anatomy,
For which I am not losing my desire, but increasing my faith,
That if I embrace the loneliness of celibacy I might celebrate love
With the same candor and reverence that I will serve to her womb,
The same place I shall come into freely for absolution,
The first place that will be the hardest to abstain from,
But for the sake of my soul, you will have to be my last addiction

Soft boar bristles brushes tangled hair
Leaving an auburn field of curls,
Straight, yet transformed, unnaturally-
Like your powdered face,
Though nominal foundation
It came not with your creation
Nor those nails or that acrylic
Your lips perfectly pink, naturally flawless,
But I barely remember a time
When your natural wonders have not
Left a red imprint on my face,
My costume, my mask,
A skin that I'm itching to shed,
You try to enhance the powers of my enemy,
When I already appreciate the beauty
Of its natural form

Soft boar bristles brushes tangled hair
Leaving an auburn field of curls,
Straight, and yet transformed, unnaturally
Like your powder face, ~~thoughts~~
Though ~~with~~ nominal foundation,
I came with your creation
It's not ~~predestined~~
Nor those nails or that acrylic
Your lips perfectly pink, naturally flawless
   But I barely remember a time
When your natural wonders have not
   Left a red imprint on my face,
My costume, my mask,
   A skin that I'm itching to shed,
You try to ~~impress by~~ enhance the powers of my enemy
When I already appreciate the beauty
   Of its natural form

A lot of women feel sorry for my love life,
Or perhaps they just feel sorry for me,
That I've chosen to outline myself in work
And brush away a social life like a pile of ash,
But I've had my fun under the red lights,
And on the dance floor a few steps from the bar
I've kissed an Apple Martini or two
Tasted Honey Brown on a brown honey,
As I let desire run across the course of my finger,
Right to the tip, where it could filter that dark space,
As a pink auditorium plays host to an audience of one
And I could be comfortable watching and performing,
But those days are done because I gave my life to God,
And that's what none of these women see,
This growth that is me, this maturation of freedom
I'm a young Booker T. Washington; Up From Slavery,
I had to let go of this condition, this mental addiction,
Of having to depend on others for happiness and sustenance,
Instead, I live for the Father because his Son died for me,
I once complained of poverty, but I let others provide for me,
And it wasn't until I left everyone alone to do it on my own,
That I realized I had two friends, no real family, and no girl,
Who could love me but me, I'm a constant evolution,
And even if parts of me have died, I'm still alive-
And in regards to my love life; don't feel sorry for it,
Be sorry that you wouldn't allow yourselves to be part of it,
Don't worry, you're beautiful, still the same, but I've changed...

She would be pious, but her prayers need not be like songs,
Yet, pure as sunlight cast blindly on others, focused on some,
Those not afraid to step out of shadow, into the blessed serenity
That comes with worshiping God by the teachings of Jesus Christ,
First and foremost, this is what I need from her, followed closely by
Kind words, that knows no malice or hatred, only encouragement,
Reinforced by the love she has for herself, like a perpetual breeze
Indiscriminately touching everyone bound by nature, alas,
This is the alpha of all beauty, transcending all shades of Black,
Brown, Yellow- any color that would bring life to her skin,
Unless, that is, her skin be without pigment, and blood be like a rose
Blooming throughout her veins, until her stem folds back into soft earth,
I need not describe any further a look or a style, because it will be her own,
And I will appreciate her for it, because history would have made her,
And growth accompanies change even as some courses remain study,
True as the principles she will have to value- virginity, though I have not,
An unfortunate hypocrisy lost because of self-control, yet, we are all sinners
That must repent and ask forgiveness, it is his will that has been made,
And at the end of the day, I want a woman that believes we are one,
Based on reciprocal actions expressed daily as the love for God's word

At times, I hold back of myself,
Like a child circling a cul-de-sac,
Watching cars zoom past street signs
Bicycle wheels eager to roll over blacktop,
But what of the black ice, potholes, or pedestrians
What of the pitfalls, what of the dangers,
What of myself, the introverted extrovert
Scribbling over the margin to live inside the page

It doesn't always have to be about love, does it,
Her eyes suggested as a snowball pounded me,
She looked sort of cute in her little snow boots,
Cream coat with large buttons, and Sno Bunny Hat,
She was just a kid, not much more than 15 or 16,
Though her outfit might have suggested otherwise
She was more of a tomboy than a young lady,
And antagonizing me was her favorite pastime,
"No woman's gonna want to be with you anyway,
You are too soft" she affectionately punctuated....
"Snowball, right to the face," I heard her say,
Perhaps she was right, I was in the middle of war
Mumbling sorted fragments of future sentences
That would express my openness to accept love,
As I was dying of frostbite and rocks in snow
Pelting me like I owed her tomorrow's lunch money,
Yet, to show her my bravery and my courage,
I took the blows with nothing but a t-shirt on,
I ran to her swiftly, kicking her square in the pants,
I sat on her back with her face planted in snow,
And I asked her, "who's soft now, who's soft now,"
She relented, admitting that she was soft, as I let go,
"I hate you," she moaned, as I walked away breathless,
"Well, it doesn't always have to be about love, does it"

This winter melody

Of wind whipping the sides of houses

Where inside fires are crackling

And kids' coats zip upwards

Hats slap on heads, hands struggle into gloves,

Doors swing open before house alarms are turned off

Icicles crash on driveways ,

As moon boots crunch through snow,

Jingling keys turn car engines,

Last gasp of mechanic roar,

Snow blowers blanketing the sound

Of steam rising from yellow liquid

Children's spirits flapping their wings

Imprinting snow angels with hand drawn halos

The second scoop of a snowman's body plops

On the first, elementary construction workers

Take a break to gulp Pepsi, as caps twist,

And pop hisses, carbon splashes around tooth enamel

Dobermans bark, as chain leashes rattle chain fences

Porch lights flick on, and children march back inside

This broken songbird

Calling out to a deaf wind,

As a herd ends with a cloud of dust

The whisper of life falls to a hush

Of a baby's breath,

Oh, if Jupiter was as small as a fireball

The fragility of nature could be understood,

How purity, pleasure, and delight

Could be a wingless flight

Of inner destruction

What good is interruption

If pause does not come with peace

Chances are I'm still awake
Sitting in the chariot of night
Sketching in some modern hieroglyph
What happiness would be like if we were together,
Something like floating from star to star
Leaving footprints as we ascend heaven's stairwell,
And should we diminish a constellation's shine
Then let those falling stars serve as a reminder
That some beauties may fade from its innate splendor,
But if you wish upon love, its light can never be lost,
How childlike, thinking of you when you're not here
Wishing you'd appear from an inkling of imagining,
Where I could hold you close as we both face forward
Towards whatever future may appear in a wisp of air,
Maybe your spirit can show me the way,
As my heart feels for you- a cautious extension,
Because where I want to be led, not many know how to get,
And even if torches are lit, it's easy to forget love's its own light,
So as you arise with the dawn, let your beauty linger on the horizon,
Chances are I'm still awake, waiting on the morning of your love

Chances are I'm still awake
Sitting in the chariot of night
Sketching in some modern hieroglyph
What happiness would be like if we were together,
~~Like floating from star to star, leaving footprints as we descend~~
Something like floating from star to star
Leaving footprints as we ascend heaven's stairwell
And should we ~~cause that star~~ deeming a constellation ~~be to~~ shine
Then let that falling star serve as a reminder
That ~~although~~ some ~~beauty~~ beauties may fade from its innate splendor
But if you wish upon love its light can never be lost,
How childlike, ~~But I am~~ thinking of you when you're not here
Wishing you were here from an inkling of imagining
And I could hold you close as we both face forward
Towards whatever future may appear in a wisp of air
Maybe ~~to~~ your spirit can show me the way ~~together for you~~
As my heart feels for you – a cautious extension
Because where I want to be led, not many know how to get
And even if torches are lit, it's easy to forget love's it's own light
So as you arise with the dawn, let your beauty linger on the horizon
Chances are I'm still awake, waiting on an invitation to the morning of your love

The right words have been scouring my mind's marshes
Looking to land on the fertile field of conscious thought,
As the early A.M. creeps into the marrow of my stamina
Causing my eyelids to linger lazily on the bottom lashes,
Yet, as I allow my sight to flourish beyond a mere squint
The evolution of your spatial beauty, luscious pink lips,
Visible inklings of divinity sparkling on your white smile,
Smooth skin wrapping your curvaceous figure in splendor
Binds the perfect frame to the continuum of a beautiful soul,
And I pray that the keepers of eternity let you pass the time
By grazing each person you meet with a wisp of your spirit,
Because your light is enamored with the blessings of God,
And it's selfish to some degree, but if time paused for me,
I'd let snowflakes dance with gravity as I'd hold your hand
And walk with you to any destination that you want to go to
Just to get to know you better than the years have allowed...
Just to see you now, to make a hammock of your warm arms
And be assured the world above us would have a similar feel,
I'd forsake the dreams of a callow heart, lay to rest false pursuits,
And pray to be that man that you have been praying God send

I've looked at you for a couple days now,
Wondering what relief or insights
You might hold in your lined pages
That will keep me coming back to you,
Right now I need you to understand,
Understand and bear with the fact, I'm in love,
So I might scribble or doodle,
Or draw stars and hearts,
Or engrave the word LOVE margin to margin
Hoping through repetition I will learn,
Historically, I have been a poor student
Failing myself through selfishness,
Letting the lives of women that have cared for me
Parachute through air with no ground to land on
Too busy taking care of me, too concerned with loving myself
To notice another life wanting to shower a greater love on me
I admit, I wasn't the man I thought I was
Too consumed with finding the right words
Instead of words that correctly portrayed how I felt,
I was a motivational speaker with an audience of one,
How could I get a girl to like me
Without really caring to see if I could love her

There is a girl I could see myself loving
In fact, in small ways I already do,
She understands the importance of words
Because she chooses her carefully with me
Never giving me too much, never giving me too little
But endowing me with a feeling,
Not of being courted or conquered
But of continuity and commitment,
Through her I feel renewed and restored,
Reborn, a passion rekindled,
I love her honesty,
Because a promise becomes a simple thing
Reinforced by holding her hand,
Or closing our eyes when we kiss,
I love that she feels safe with me,
And comfortable enough to tell me when I'm wrong
Even when I feel justified in my thinking,
And I've been thinking, starting out as friends
Was/Is probably the best thing for us,
Not to mention the best thing for love
And that's what I really want from her
The feeling, not just the word

At night, I wish I could grab a handful of stars,
And bring the light of the universe to your doorstep,
Because an angel deserves nothing less than Heaven,
But I can't even afford the jewels of this Earth,
Not those diamond earrings, pearl necklaces, or
Platinum bracelets- and I've seen you smile
While your breath slips away as you window shop,
And all I've got is my word- baby, one day, I swear-
But right now I'm working this job that gives me a check
That makes me question why I get up this early in the AM,
As I look in the refrigerator for water and a slice of bread
I understand why- life's hard, I walk to work, no car,
I'm just trying to make it, and today I wanted to see your face,
But there is no way for me to make it across town, so now
I'm alone in my room listening to love songs
That says if your heart is hurting, don't waste your time,
When I get a text from you, "sorry we didn't have a chance
2 talk 2day. I kinda had a bad day 2day..."
Me too, I couldn't be there for you, and your heart is not content,
Something has replaced your happiness with tiny tears,
And if our souls were mirrors, you'd see I feel the same way,
So I'm going to have to let you go, because you deserve better,
Better than what I can offer, more than what I can give,
Though I did want you to live in the mansion of my heart
Where I could lasso the moon and bring it to your window

~~It's not end of these days~~
~~That day brings the hundreds to grow he different~~

At night I wish I could grab a handful of stars
And bring the light of the universe to your doorstep
Because an angel deserves nothing less than heaven
But I can't even afford the jewels of this Earth
Not those diamond earrings, pearl necklaces or
Platinum bracelets, - and I've seen you smile
While your breath slips away as you window shop,
And all I've got is my word - baby one day, I swear
But right now I'm working this job that gives me a check
That makes me question why I get up this early in the AM,
As I look in the refrigerator for water and slice of bread
I understand why, life's hard, I walk to work, no car,
I'm just trying to make it, and today I wanted see your face
But there was no way for me to make it across town, so now
I'm alone in my room listening to love songs
That says if your heart is hurting, don't waste your time,
When I get a text from you, "sorry we didn't have a chance
2 talk 2day. I kinda had a bad day 2day." - Me too,
I couldn't be there for you, and your heart is not content,
Something has replaced your happiness with tiny tears;
And if our souls were mirrors, you'd see I feel the same way
So I'm have to let you go because you deserve better,
Better than what I can offer, more than what I can give,
Though I'd'd want see you the way, and also love

I never caught her eye like the billboards do
Lofts, condos in high-rises, 100-200k to live by a cloud
I was closer to the street signs, bus stops and crosswalks
And she was too, but to her that lamppost was a palm tree,
And the overpass by the freeway to her was a breezeway
A lookout to blue skies and oceans, none specific, just beyond me
Or my type, another guy hoping to glide into the tide of her waters,
I guess there are no men in paradise, just girls who dream better tomorrows

But maybe there is a boy with a wilted heart standing in the yard
Waiting for his grandparents to come home to attend to their garden
Knowing they are now part of the landscaping; I shuffle tiny rocks,
My back against an elm tree, faith asks me to carve its name in the bark,
I oblige for some future resident will see if they kneel by the root,

She wears those designer boots with long zippers, black skirts, pretty blouses
And hangs out in lounges with a smokey haze, glasses- red wine filled,
Perhaps a Corona or two- bottlenecks tap together in pleasure of the night
As she shifts, she moves, a slightly better view around a burgundy Kangol cap,
A familiar face standing in a white light, just like those nights by the bus stop,
And she remembers those palm trees, and she remembered me, and wondered,
How did I get on this stage?

I pressed a finger on the doorbell, inviting an orange glow

Followed by an orchestrated series of noises for a signal,

As I waited beyond the cedar frame, I looked down,

The outline of a welcome mat gnarled my senses,

I surveyed the yard- unkempt grass, an assortment of dry leaves,

I made an unassuming sidestep towards a window unhappy with itself,

A loss of transparency, I gave it back some of its dignity

Brushing away the grime from the center of its pane,

I sat in the stained outline with my jeans as a seat

Pondering over the petals of red roses, the veins of life we bled together;

Every kiss was a struggle- you tried to identify truth with cushioned lips

I surveyed passion with the delicacies of French

Inspired by the precedent of language presented to me,

I desired to taste your love, while you yearned to feel mine fill you

We disagreed on interpretation as calendar days became X's,

My eyes wandered to the sidewalk, by the edge of a tattered couch,

Its seats weighted down with black trash bags engulfed in debris,

A mangled red tri-cycle sits off balanced by a battered metallic can,

A gutter deflated a kid's dream of leaving his mother's hand,

That same touch that used to covet mine as an equal to her son,

And while she sought a family, I sifted through shades of my past

To decipher I was a cipher siphoning happiness to my heart from her womb

I would never blame my life on anyone,
With a clear mind my choices have been made
By the person who chooses to live by consequence,
Myself, I have been open to let down
And prone to give up,
I believed I could fly while I was in free fall
Never bothering to spread my wings,
Hoping to absorb the crash and the aftermath
With the same blind faith
That I can survive more than I will live,
I often wonder what majesty lies beyond here
When the tunnel closes and the Light looms large,
And a small world becomes an endless Universe
Will my inner being have as much Lumina as the stars,
This little Earth, where treachery lurks in our hearts
To despise the will of our souls,
Where pride takes hold, and we have only ourselves to please,
I want to be able to give my life with no ambition
Other than to please God, when Heaven calls

## When Heaven Calls

I would never blame my life on anyone
With a clear mind my choices have been made
By the person who chooses to live by consequence,
Myself, I have been open to let down
And prone to give up,
I believed I could fly while I was in free fall
Never bothering to spread my wings,
Hoping to absorb the crash and aftermath
With the same blind faith
That I can survive more than I will live,
I often wonder what majesty lies beyond here
When the tunnel and the light looms large,
And a small world an endless Universe
Will my inner being have as much Lumina as the stars,
This little Earth, where treachery lurks in our hearts
To despise the will of our souls,
Where pride takes hold, and we have only ourselves to please,
I want to be able to give my life with no ambition
Other than to please God, when Heaven Calls

I was born with nothing but the skin on the top of my head,

Seasoned with soft brown curly locks over time

When kempt and cut lay flat on my scalp,

The gourmet of beautiful genes my parents mixed within me

Overcoming the segregation of thought that blacks and whites

Could never come together, I am here as a reminder of history,

The will of men is not of equal strength with the will of nature

For the narrowness of my nose and the fullness of my lips

Are the products of different continents merged here-

In my America, a land that was pillaged and then bought

To constutionalize a dream to be amended by Abe, then Martin,

And a host of others, who refused to succumb to civil war or unrest

So even if shot to death, I could still bleed the story of many nations

Into the land of the natives...but nothing malicious needs to happen

For every day I am dying- gravity aging skin I try to fight with vitamins,

Vitamin D we get from the sun, taken in a cancer capsule,

Is it worth the hassle, to give my skin a little more pigment

In tribute to the color that my ancestors died for, on both sides,

Tanning only to become pale again at the moment of death,

Only for the mortician to add color to a once vibrant flesh...

Seems like a constant celebration of the Lord's creation

So even if I stepped outside of my race, dictated by man,

To have a woman of a different classification fertilize my seed

I would take comfort knowing that she was still pulled from the rib

Not from a certain type of melanin or albino gene,

And our child too could be like us, indifferent to our coverings,

But in tune to our internal workings, some may define as spirit,

Because one day our organs will fail, and our hearts will stop,

And our souls will be ushered into houses we've made with our good deeds,

So I hope my child gets a good foundation from me, because every day I'm dying...

*Dedicated to my Best Friend and his Girlfriend...it's not about race...it's about LOVE! I can't wait to see your child come into the world*

When I was a child, I would do things to please my curiosity,
Like the day I decided to swing on the bank's curtains
While you were talking to a representative about your account,
And I would hear you warily calling my name,
More out of concern than embarrassment,
And there I was, a few inches above the ground, with a grand smile,
Hey, Grandma look at me, with the innocence of accomplishment,
You ushered me to your side for safekeeping, and damage control,
But never was I threatened, or did I feel a sense of shame for wrong
I was counseled by comfort, never admonished or outcast,
Yet, since you've passed, there have been no Brach's peppermints,
Or grape or orange lollipops with joyous eyes at my boyish wonder,
I just wonder if I have disappointed you with things I've said or done,
Now that Heaven has augmented your senses by blunting your life
And you can focus on me, like you used to do with the nightly news,
Pondering the world from your queen bed, my life's your news cycle-
I'm not afraid to admit I have no idea where I am going,
I'm just walking through open doors without hellos or good-byes,
My manners like soiled bed sheets I continue to sleep in,
I only speak when I have to...Grandma, this time I'm calling your name

3.) While you were talking to a representative about your account,
4.) And I would hear you warily calling my name,
5.) More out of concern than embarrassment,
6.) And there I was a few inches above the ground with a grand smile,
7.) Hey, grandma, look at me, with the innocence of accomplishment,
8.) You ushered me to your side for safe keeping, and damage control,
9.) But never was I threatened, or did I feel a sense of shame for wrong
10.) I was counseled by comfort, never admonished or outcast,
11.) Yet, since you've passed there has been no Brach's peppermints
12.) Or, grape or orange lollipops with joyous eyes at my boyish wonder,
13.) I just wonder if I have disappointed you, with things I've said or done,
14.) Now that Heaven has augmented your senses by blunting your life
15.) And you can focus on me, like you used to do with the nightly news
16.) Pondering the ~~~~~ bed, my life your news cycle;
17.) I'm not afraid to admit I have no idea where I am going,
18.) I'm just walking through open doors without hellos or goodbyes,
19.) My manners like soiled bedsheets I continue to sleep.
~~I only speak when I have to, and to respond, only your death my name~~
20.) I only speak when I have to... Grandma, this time, I'm calling you name

I've prayed on it in the quiet quarters of my room
My knees red from kneeling, my head on clinched hands,
I'm ready now, to take this next step and invite love in,
I wouldn't waste your time Lord, if my heart were half-filled,
I wouldn't let my words titter on the edge of a fickle desire,
And I know this may take some time to hear of your response,
But when you give me your answer, I know that I'll be pleased,
Because I know the woman you send would have been sent for me

I'm ready now, unlike before, when I was still searching for myself
Then, I was unrelenting in my unwillingness for companionship,
I believed romance to be a string of fantastical casual encounters,
Memorable nights with forgettable faces, building my legend,
But as the hero of my own lore, I'd become my own nemesis,
And nothing sounds worse than an echo of applause
When you're the only one standing championing your own cause,
So of all my flaws, this is where I'd first like to make a change

Lord, I come to you with humility, because I am your child,
Let your will be done, dear Lord, because I am ready now

[~~Somedays I just go through the motions~~]
[~~The same routine of the same things~~]

~~I wish to God that you were just another person to walk in my life~~

## I'm Ready Now

I've prayed on it in the quiet quarters of my room
My knees red from kneeling, my head on clinched hands,
I'm ready now, to take this next step and invite love in,
I wouldn't waste your time Lord, if my heart were half-filled,
I wouldn't let my words titter on the edge of a fickle desire,
And I know this may take some time to hear of your response,
But when you give me your answer, I know that I'll be pleased,
Because I know the woman you send would have been sent for me

I'm Ready now, unlike before, when I was still searching for myself
Then, I was unrelenting in my unwillingness for companionship,
I believed romance to be a string of fantastical encounters,
Memorable nights with forgettable faces, building my legend,
But as the hero of my own lore, I'd become my own nemesis,
And nothing sounds worse than an echo of applause
When you've the only one standing championing your own cause,
So of all my flaws, this is where I'd first like to make a change

Lord, I come to you with humility, because I am your child
Let your will be done, dear Lord, I am ready now.

Sometimes we dream of things we can't remember

And they are left trapped somewhere in a void,

The slightest noise can destroy a kingdom, clip a wing,

Or make the petals from a flower fall

Before it ever reaches a lovers hand,

And the scenes that expanded from the fast sketch of eyes

Quicksand into the unknown, as we're paralyzed by the sun,

Scratching our head for memories bound to only one,

But lately there has been a trend where dreams don't end,

Instead they tend to come to me in bits and flashes,

And are extended safe passage from eyes closed to eyes open

That's what the smile in your picture seems to remind me

Everything I ever wanted can be contained in 5ft.

The inches are of no concern, I can find the remainder in your eyes,

How can I not remember how I felt inside,

The depth of joy from the briefest moment in your arms

That first night I took to bed that feeling with me,

And as my heart swelled during the night for weeks

Finally, on this morning, my heart pours out to you,

Today's the first time I woke up still dreaming about love

Twilight bore down the highway

The stars already loomed large

I swore we were going to drive off the edge of the Earth

In a car that was almost a decade old and in need of an oil change,

Yet, the road continued on, up a hill, down a hill, and around a mountain

I glanced down at you to see if you were still sleeping,

Or just enjoying the moment,

Your eyes remained closed, as you sat sidesaddle in my lap,

It was almost as if your breath mimicked the silence of the open road,

And wherever your mind took you, peace was painted on its landscape,

You barely moved your head as it rested on my shoulder,

I couldn't resist planting a soft kiss on your forehead, as I stroked your hair,

Cliché as written romances may go, but it felt right, so I went for it,

Hoping to stir your thoughts with the love I have for you,

It's hard to believe that neither of us has said the word to the other,

But, for what it's worth, I've been wanting to tell you how I've felt for months,

It's just...where do I begin...

How does a man deliver love to a woman with a simple sentence,

How could you take it without question,

How amazing would it be if love were like a star, and all could tell by its glow

Never has love been so frightening

That at the sight of you I walk away,

Quickly, with each step, as if to say

I'm not good enough to be in your presence

I'm not worthy enough to stand in your grace,

And at the slightest intimation of your face

I seek a lesser gratification

Than the smile you unveil to me,

I speak to you weary of my metallic words,

Knowing rust can deteriorate strength,

Just as action can nullify intent,

As if I passed you by and reached for your shadow,

I want you to be in my life,

But never have I been so afraid to love

I was so impressed by my divinity
Enjoying my invincibility against the world
I breathed without worry, convincingly,
Until the day my heart was taken by a girl

I tumbled to the Earth
And asked the God over me
How could this be

He smiled through his sun
As my anguish began to recede

What type of god could I be
If I did not know love

What type of man was I
If I did not know pain

How could I have known myself if it weren't for you

The orphan moon sat close to the Earth
Too young to be alone in this big universe,
As I looked with eyes wide at the night sky
Watching raindrops paralyze movement
Of creatures below wanting to stay dry,
But how could I, so saturated by my surroundings
Be lured into the coziness of the indoors
When my heart yearned to explore the forces of nature,
My shirt stuck to me like moist paper on a piece of candy
And I fancied the warm liquid on my face,
Dripping from the tip of my nose to my lips,
As I thought of her words just after her kiss,
"Baby, I'm in love with you"...
I wonder if I imagined it all, now that I am here
To recount the evening that was,
I check my arms for goose bumps induced by her touch,
And they are still uniform on the surface,
My skin armed in defense that my heart may need,
But when I take a small step, I feel a breath in a breeze
"Baby, you can believe in me"...

## You Can Believe In Me

The orphan moon sat close to the Earth
Too young to be alone in this big universe
As I looked with eyes wide at the night sky
Watching raindrops paralyze movement
Of creatures below wanting to stay dry.
But how could I, so saturated by my surroundings
Be lured into the coziness of the indoors
When my heart yearned to explore the forces of nature,
My shirt stuck to me like moist paper on a piece of candy
And I fancied the warm liquid on my face,
Dripping from the tip of my nose to my lips,
As I thought of her words, just after her kiss,
"Baby, I'm in love with you..."
I wonder if I imagined it all, now that I am here
To recount the evening that was,
I check my arms for goosebumps induced by her touch
And they are still uniformed on the surface
My skin armed in defense that my heart may need
But when I take a small step, I feel a breath in a breeze
"Baby, you can believe in me"...

I want to get to know you in all the ways that matter to you,
Because it is not my intent for you to just be in my life,
I want to be involved in yours- encouraging your dreams,
Strengthening your weaknesses- so that on your bad days
You can sit in your sweatshirt without make-up if you want
And we can talk about feelings you would write in a diary,
I will not turn the volume of the radio over your problems,
Whatever is on TV can wait as long as you are in front of me,
Because you're the wish list of everything I've ever wanted,
And I'm going to be your protector, your provider, your King
If you allow me to sit in the throne of your cherished heart
I will never be the cause of your misery, or author your pains
I'll be the source of your happiness, I will extend you my name,
So you will never have to ask yourself if I am finally the one,
Because we shall be one- but I first need you to open up to me,
In order to get to know you in all the ways that matter to you

Sitting in the corner of the windowsill
Watching the western sun rise to the east
The side of my face warming with panes of glass
How fast has my heart melted with night's frost,
My pink fingertips desire the inside of my sleeves,
My eyes long to keep moving over waves of cedar trees,
I haven't been to sleep in days, lost to the sway of nature,
Using a knuckle, I draw a small heart out of moisture
I see life in my creation as light reigns in the open gap,
I'm in love and I know it, and this is all I can do to show it,
I'm so in awe of you wonder has limited me to insomnia
Seeing your face in every cloud, I could be crazy be now,
But I'm going to pick the petals from every flower in the field,
Sprinkle them on the floor, lay them on the bedspread,
I'll garden romance with the aromas that remind me of you
Sweet and gentle, with the right amount of longevity
To keep me lingering even when you are long gone,
I remove myself from the windowsill to dive into clean linen
Rolling around until glitter on the ceiling becomes starlight,
I'm so in love I can no longer tell the sheets from the blinds

Let's sample the Divine,

And reach within ourselves to give life to love,

We can color it like the feathers of a macaw-

Scarlet, blue and gold, or we can invent palettes

Never waxed on a crayon or mixed into paint,

And while we do that, let's give love a meaning,

One that is longer than the reach of the stars

But simplified to who we are; and who are we-

We are spiritual artist, we are the creators of love,

Proprietors of infinite space to let our child evolve

Over markers of time, charting life to death's border,

Where we can watch love spread its colorful wings

And lift its being into the realms of eternity,

This is what I want with you, what I want from you,

To make something beautiful, to know that it is ours,

And to be admired from afar even if never understood,

But even if no one noticed I'd still want you, and only you,

Because I know if I somehow became the last man on Earth

The Divine would pull your growth from the side of me,

And if I returned inside of you, how could we not make love

I think God handpicked your Lumina like wild flowers
From various fields of light at the onset of creation,
And seasoned your brilliance with truth from the Spirit
As He allowed you to develop in Heaven for a time
Until He deemed you were ready to come one April,
And from that age of newborn youth to today's conclusion
You have upheld that vision of growth and unique beauty
That if you were placed anywhere else in the universe
You would be the same benevolent being that you are today
Because God, in all his magnificence, made you that way,
And it's not the temerity of heart that guides my words,
But sincerity woven in my creation that speaks on my behalf,
Because I love you- not as in like or as, no similes or metaphors,
No special cadences, or lavish adjectives, just simply, I Love You-
I can no better explain it than I could the magic of our blood
Animating our hearts so that we may be conscious of existence,
Both yours and mine, so that when I write you shall read
And reread, until you become so versed in my works
That you understand I am my word, and my word is of you,
So that if words were not spoken then you would know
That I could still hand pick your light like wild flowers

Destiny has done its part now that we have met,
Shall we forfeit the industry of those who've kept us alive
Those who have clothed us, fed us, given us shelter,
And educated us so we are able to communicate intelligently,
Is it fair to ask for blessings if we allow access to our hearts
Knowing the potential we have for love and resist our future
Based on our past, or the doubts the world has given us
That if truth is too good it must be inherently false,
Tell me that we are not so blind that we walk a straight path
And wonder where to turn- tell me we'll not always be sheep,
The worst thing we can do is to feel that we aren't deserving,
As if happiness is only for those who have followed a formula,
Made all the right choices, and followed legacies left for them,
That is what makes us special, that we are chance takers,
Big dreamers, willing to make our vulnerability our strength,
We live the lives we have chosen, though destiny has its part,
Tell me please that we recognize now that the onus is on us
That if we believe that we are meant to be- it shall be,
And if we neglect all the efforts made on our behalf
No one is to blame but ourselves, destiny has done its part

Take away my heart if this is not love
Like winter does the color from fall,
Because I never want to be deceived
Into thinking you are merely a season,
That an emotional investment could be lost
With the ease that time moves it hands,
I want you to be my personal Heaven,
My private forever, my everlasting inspiration,
And the sole reason my soul longs to exist,
To have witnessed nothingness materialize love
Is the feeling taken from words galvanizing light
At the genesis of sight from my eyes to yours,
I never want to be without you again, to that I swear,
So when I say amen I have to say it again
In affirmation of love, that I'm in it, and thankful for it,
The want of moving forward with you by my side
Is only a proposal, but one that I ask from you…
If you could set aside disbelief to take hold of my love
I promise to never make you regret the yes to this question,
Will you marry me?

## The Proposal

Take away my heart if this is not love
Like winter does the color from fall
Because I never want to be deceived
Into thinking you are merely a season,
That an emotional investment could be lost
With the ease that time moves its hands,
I want you to be my personal Heaven,
My private forever, my everlasting inspiration
And the sole reason my soul longs to exist,
To have witnessed nothingness materialize love
Is the feeling taken from words galvanizing light
At the genesis of sight from my eyes to yours,
I never want to be without you again, to that I swear,
So when I say amen I have to say it again
In affirmation of love, that I am in it, and thankful for it,
The want of moving forward with you by my side
Is only a proposal, but one that I ask from you...
I promise to never make you regret the yes to this question,
Will you marry me?

www.ingramcontent.com/pod-product-compliance
Lightning Source LLC
Chambersburg PA
CBHW060813010526
44117CB00002B/24